"Ai"
your assistant for financial independence

Author : Dr.SZ
24.04.2024

"Artificial Intelligence: Your assistant to Financial Independence"

'It is financial independence itself'

""Get started with Me now ""

I hope you enjoy reading

Dr.SZ

Introduction.................
- The Importance of Artificial Intelligence in the Modern Era - An Overview of AI and Its Role in Achieving Financial Independence
- Objectives and Structure of the Book
- Target Audience.

.........Chapter 1: Understanding Artificial Intelligence and Its History.......

1.1 Defining Artificial Intelligence
- A simple definition of artificial intelligence.
- Examples of basic AI applications.

1.2 The History of Artificial Intelligence - The evolution of AI from its inception. - Key historical milestones.

1.3 Pioneers in Artificial Intelligence
- Notable figures in the AI field.
- Their achievements and impact.

1.4 Types of Artificial Intelligence
- Narrow AI vs. General AI.
- Examples and uses of each type.

1.5 Early Applications of Artificial Intelligence
- The first practical applications of AI.
- The impact these early applications had.

1.6 The Rapid Development of Artificial Intelligence - Factors contributing to the rapid advancement of AI. - Examples of recent AI applications.

1.7 Future Predictions for Artificial Intelligence
- Future visions for AI development.
- Its potential impacts on our lives.

Chapter 2: Artificial Intelligence in the Economy ....

2.1 The Role of AI in the Global Economy.
- The impact of AI on global markets.
- Examples of AI use in major corporations.

2.2 AI in Local Economic Sectors
- AI applications in local industries.
- Examples and case studies of local implementations.

2.3 AI in Financial Sectors
- The use of AI in asset management and finance.
- Examples of intelligent financial systems.

2.4 AI in Stock Markets
- AI applications in trading and speculation.
- Examples of trading algorithms.

2.5 AI and Personal Investment
- How to use AI to improve investment decisions.
- Free tools to achieve financial independence.

2.6 AI and the Digital Economy
- The role of AI in the development of the digital economy.

2.7 The Impact of AI on Traditional Jobs
- The challenges AI poses to the job market.
- How to adapt to these changes.

........Chapter 3: Artificial Intelligence in Security and Defense...........

3.1 AI in National Security
- The role of AI in enhancing internal security.
- Examples of AI-based security systems.

3.2 AI in Military Defense
- AI applications in military equipment and systems. - Examples of drones and military robots.

3.3 AI in Intelligence Gathering
- AI applications in intelligence data collection.
- Examples of smart systems for security analysis.

3.4 Protecting Critical Infrastructure with AI
- The role of AI in safeguarding energy and communicationinfrastructures.
- Examples of systems protecting critical infrastructure.

3.5 Combating Terrorism with AI
- How AI helps in identifying terrorist threats.
- Examples of AI programs used in counterterrorism.

3.6 AI and International Cooperation in Security
- International collaboration in AI for security purposes.
- Examples of international initiatives.

3.7 Ethical Challenges of Using AI in Security and Defense
- Discussion of ethical issues related to AI use in security.
- Case studies and international stances.

......Chapter 4: Artificial Intelligence in Everyday Life..........

4.1 AI in Transportation
- Self-driving cars and smart transportation applications.
- Examples of leading companies in this field.

4.2 AI in Home Services
- Home robots and smart assistants.
- Examples of smart home devices.

4.3 AI in Healthcare
- The use of AI in diagnosis and treatment.
- Examples of AI tools in hospitals.

4.4 AI in Education
- AI applications in enhancing education.
- Examples of smart learning systems.

4.5 AI in Social Media
- How AI changes our interaction on social media platforms.
- Examples of systems that analyze and guide social content.

4.6 AI in Entertainment and Arts
- AI applications in music and film production.
- Examples of artistic works created by AI.

4.7 AI in Shopping and E-commerce
- How AI is used to improve the shopping experience.
- Examples of websites and apps relying on AI.

............Chapter 5: AI and Financial Independence.........

5.1 How AI Can Achieve Financial Independence
- Strategies for using AI to generate income.
- Examples of success stories.

5.2 AI Tools for Generating Passive Income
- Applications and systems that generate income withoutcontinuous effort.
- Examples of free and paid tools.

5.3 AI in E-commerce
- How to benefit from AI in online selling.
- Examples of smart e-commerce tools.

5.4 AI and Remote Work
- How AI facilitates remote work.
- Examples of companies that rely on AI for remote operations.

5.5 Investing in Artificial Intelligence
- How to invest in AI companies to generate profits.
- Examples of successful AI startups.

5.6 AI and Time Management
- Using AI applications to improve personal productivity.
- Examples of apps that help organize time.

5.7 AI and Personal Marketing
- How AI can help build personal branding.
- Examples of tools that make self-marketing easier.

Chapter 6: AI and Society:........

6.1 The Impact of AI on the Job Market
- Changes in the job market due to AI.
- How to adapt to these changes.

6.2 AI in Education
- How AI contributes to improving education quality.
- Examples of smart educational initiatives.

6.3 AI in Public Services
- The role of AI in improving government services.
- Examples of AI applications in the public sector.

6.4 AI in Medicine and Healthcare
- How AI is changing the future of healthcare.
- Examples of medical AI applications.

6.5 AI and the Environment
- Using AI to improve natural resource management.
- Examples of applications in agriculture and energy.

6.6 AI in Humanitarian Aid
- The role of AI in enhancing crisis response.
- Examples of AI projects that have provided rapid and effectivehumanitarian aid.

6.7 AI and Humanitarian Assistance

- The Role of AI in Crisis Response
- How AI is used in data analysis to prioritize humanitarianefforts.
- Examples of AI projects that have rapidly and effectivelydelivered humanitarian assistance.
- Big Data Analysis in Disaster Management
- The role of AI in improving disaster planning and response. - Examples of systems that help predict disasters and mitigatetheir effects.
- Smart Applications in Humanitarian Relief
- Using AI in the fair distribution of aid and resources.
- Examples of AI tools used in the field to track and coordinaterelief operations.
- Technology and Privacy in Humanitarian Work
- Discussing privacy challenges and ethics in the use of AI inhumanitarian work.

- Case studies where AI was used in ways that raised ethicalquestions.
- AI and International Cooperation in Crises

 - How AI can enhance international cooperation in crisismanagement.
- Examples of joint projects between countries andhumanitarian organizations that have benefited from AI.
-AI Applications in Reconstruction
- The role of AI in rebuilding communities after disasters. - Examples of initiatives for reconstruction using AI.
- The Future of AI in Humanitarian Work
- Future outlook on the role of AI in improving humanitarianefforts.
- New technologies expected and their potential impact onhumanitarian aid.

Chapter 7: AI in Cultural and Artistic..... Fields

7.1 AI in Music

- Analyzing Musical Patterns
- How AI contributes to analyzing music and understandingsound patterns.
- Examples of artificial music generation systems.
- Creating Music with AI
- AI applications in composing music.
- Examples of musical works entirely created by AI.
- Enhancing Music Production with AI
- How AI can improve the quality of music production. - Tools and software that assist musicians using AI.

7.2 AI in Visual Arts

- Generating Digital Art
- Using AI to produce paintings and artworks.
- Examples of artists using AI in their creations. - Human-Machine Interaction in Arts
- How artists interact with AI to produce new works.
- Examples of collaborative art projects between humans andAI.

7.3 AI in Cinema
- Film Production with AI
- How AI aids in editing and producing films.
- Examples of films produced with the help of AI
. - Analyzing Scripts and Actors' Performances
- Using AI to improve scripts and direct actors' performances.
- AI tools that assist in writing scripts.

7.4 AI in Literature and Publishing
- Creating Literary Texts
- How AI can contribute to writing stories and novels.
- Examples of books authored with the help of AI.
- Analyzing Literary Texts
- Using AI to analyze classical and modern literary works.
- Tools that help understand and interpret literature.

7.5 AI in Digital Games
- Developing Games with AI
- How AI contributes to the development of digital games.
- Examples of games that rely on AI.
- Personalizing the Gaming Experience
- Using AI to customize the experience for players based ontheir behavior.

- Examples of AI systems in games that adapt to playing styles.

7.6 AI in Media and Publishing
- Generating Media Content
- How AI can contribute to producing news and media content.
- Examples of news sites using AI to write reports. - Analyzing Audience Reactions
- The role of AI in understanding and analyzing audiencefeedback on media content.
- Examples of AI usage in improving publishing strategies.

7.7 AI in Literary and Artistic Translation
- Improving the Quality of Literary Translation
- How AI helps in translating literary and artistic texts withhigh quality.
- Examples of advanced translation systems that rely on AI. - Reviving Classical Literary Works
- The role of AI in translating and modernizing old literaryworks.
- Examples of projects utilizing AI to republish classicliterature in new languages.

Conclusion…………………….

Introduction:
In the rapidly evolving landscape of the 21st century, few innovations have had as profound an impact as Artificial Intelligence (AI).
As it permeates nearly every aspect of ourlives, AI has shifted from being a futuristic concept to anessential component of modern society.
Whether it's optimising business processes, enhancing medical diagnostics, or revolutionising transportation, AI's influence is undeniable. However, beyond these broad applications, AI holds a uniquepotential: it can be a powerful tool for individuals seeking financial independence.
This book, "Artificial Intelligence: Your way to Financial Independence", aims to explore how AI can be harnessed to achieve just that.

The Importance of Artificial Intelligence in the Modern Era: Artificial Intelligence has become a cornerstone of innovation, driving significant advancements across industries.

Its ability toprocess vast amounts of data, learn from patterns, and make decisions with minimal human intervention has made it indispensable in today's world.

From automating routine tasks to enabling break throughs in scientific research, AI's applications are diverse and ever-expanding.

Yet, its importance extends beyond large-scale industries; AI is reshaping personal financeand creating new opportunities for individuals. As traditional paths to wealth and security evolve, AI offers new avenues forachieving financial goals, making it crucial for individuals to understand and leverage this technology in the modern era.

An Overview of AI and Its Role in Achieving Financial Independence:
The concept of financial independence.
—where one has sufficient personal wealth to live without needing to work actively.
—has been a long-standing aspiration for many.
AI hasthe potential to make this dream more attainable by providing tools and strategies that maximise income, optimise investments, and automate financial decisions.
Whether through AI-driven stock trading algorithms, personalised investment advice, or automated passive income streams, AI enables individuals to grow their wealth more efficiently than ever before.
 This book delves into these applications, offering a roadmap for readers to use AI as a means to secure their financial future.

Objectives and Structure of the Book: The primary objective of this book is to equip readers with a deep understanding of how AI can be applied to achieve financial independence. It is structured to guide readers from the foundational concepts of AI to its practical applications in personal finance.
The book begins with an exploration of AI's history and development, laying the ground work for understanding its current capabilities.
It then moves on to discuss AI's role in various sectors
—such as the economy, security, everyday life, and the arts
—before focusing on specific tools and strategies that individuals can use to build wealth. Each chapter is designed to offer both theoretical insights andpractical examples, ensuring that readers can apply the knowledge in real-world scenarios.

Target Audience:
This book is intended for a broad audience, including individuals who are new to AI and those who have a basic understanding but seek to deepen their know ledge. It is particularly suited for entrepreneurs, investors, and professionals who are interested in leveraging technology to enhance their financial standing. Additionally, the book is valuable for anyonewho is curious about the future of AI and its impact on personal and professional life. By the end of this journey, readers will not only understand the power of AI ,but also how to harness it to achieve lasting financial independence.
- Embrace Creativity and Innovation: Leverage the capabilities of AI to launch new and innovative projects. The digital worldoffers countless opportunities, and AI can be your partner increating new solutions and ideas.

- Consider Ethical Implications: Always be mindful of ethical considerations when using AI.
Ensure that you use this technology in ways that benefit society and avoid engaging in practice that may be harmful or unethical.

- Invest Time Wisely: Clearly define your goals and use AI to help you achieve them effectively. Organizing your time and investing your efforts in areas that yield the highest financial returns can have a significant impact on your success.

- Leverage Social Networks and Digital Communities: Joingroups and forums that are interested in AI and its applications.
 Learning from others' experiences and exchanging ideas can help you gain new insights and achieve greater success.
Get started >>

"Chapter 1: Understanding Artificial Intelligence and ItsHistory"

Artificial Intelligence (AI) has become an integral part of our modern world, influencing everything from the way we work and communicate to how we understand complex systems. To fully grasp the potential and implications of AI, it's essential to explore its foundations, history, key figures, and the different types that exist. This chapter provides a comprehensive over view of AI, tracing its evolution, examining its pioneers, and discussing its early and current applications, as well as future predictions.

Defining Artificial Intelligence1.1

At its core, Artificial Intelligence refers to the capability of machines to mimic or replicate intelligent human behavior.
More specifically, AI involves creating systems or algorithms that can perform tasks typically requiring human intelligence, such as learning, reasoning, problem-solving, understanding natural language, and recognizing patterns.

A Simple Definition of Artificial Intelligence: AI can be definedas the branch of computer Science focused on developing machines and software with the ability to exhibit intelligent behavior. This intelligence may manifest in various forms, including the ability to learn from data, adapt to new inputs, or make decisions with varying degrees of autonomy.

Examples of Basic AI Applications: Some of the most common examples of AI in everyday life include virtual assistants like Siri and Alexa, which use natural language processing to understand and respond to user queries. Another example is recommendation algorithms on platforms like Netflix or YouTube, which analyze user preferences and behavior to suggest relevant content. These examples illustrate how AI is seamlessly integrated into our daily routines, often without us even realizing it.

1.2 The History of Artificial Intelligence
The history of AI is a journey that spans several decades, marked by periods of optimism, significant break throughs, and moments of set back. Understanding this history helps in appreciating the complexity of AI and its development over time.

The Evolution of AI from Its Inception: The concept of machines that could think dates back to ancient mythology, but the formal study of AI began in the 1950s. British mathematician and logician Alan Turing is often credited with laying the ground work for AI with his proposal of the Turing Test in 1950, which sought to determine a machine's ability to exhibit intelligent behavior indistinguishable from that of a human.

Key Historical Milestones: One of the first milestones in AI was the 1956 Dartmouth Conference, where the term «Artificial Intelligence» was coined. Early AI research focused on symbolic reasoning and problem-solving, leading to the development of programs that could solve algebraic problems, play chess, and prove logical theorems. The 1980s saw the riseof expert systems, which were among the first successful forms of AI applied in industries, designed to replicate the decision-making abilities of human experts. The late 20th and early 21st centuries witnessed significant advancement with the advent of machine learning and neural networks, which enabled AI systems to learn from vast amounts of data, significantly improving their capabilities.

1.3 Pioneers in Artificial Intelligence

The development of AI has been shaped by numerous brilliant minds, whose contributions have had lasting impacts on thefield. These pioneers laid the foundation for the complex AI systems we see today.

Notable Figures in the AI Field: Alan Turing, often regarded as-the father of AI, was instrumental in conceptualizing the idea ofmachines simulating human intelligence. Another key figure is John McCarthy, who not only coined the term «Artificial Intelligence» but also developed the programming language LISP, which became a standard tool for AI research. Marvin Minsky, a co-founder of the MIT AI Laboratory, was a significant figure in AI research, contributing to robotics and cognitive psychology.

Their Achievements and Impact: Turing's work on the Turing Test and his theoretical contributions to computing laid the groundwork for future AI development. McCarthy's invention of LISP enabled more sophisticated AI programming, while his work on time-sharing systems contributed to the development of modern computing. Minsky's research in symbolic reasoning and neural networks influenced the direction of AI research, bridging the gap between human cognitive processes and machine capabilities.

1.4 Types of Artificial Intelligence

AI is not a monolithic technology; it exists in different forms, each with distinct capabilities and applications. Understanding the types of AI helps clarify its potential and limitations.

Narrow AI vs. General AI: Narrow AI, also known as Weak AI, refers to AI systems designed to perform a specific task or a narrow range of tasks. These systems do not possess generalised intelligence and are limited to their programmed functions. Examples include language translation services, facial recognition systems, and autonomous vehicles. In contrast, General AI, or Strong AI, refers to AI with the ability to perform any intellectual task that a human being can do. General AI remains a theoretical concept, with research ongoing to achieve this level of machine intelligence.

Examples and Uses of Each Type: Narrow AI is prevalent in many industries today. For instance, AI-powered diagnostic tools in health care can analyse medical images to detect diseases with high accuracy. In finance, AI algorithms are used to predict market trends and manage investments. General AI, while not yet realised, is the subject of much speculation, with potential uses ranging from fully autonomous robots to AI systems capable of human-like reasoning and decision-making across various domains.

1.5 Early Applications of Artificial Intelligence

The early applications of AI set the stage for its current widespread use. These initial for ays into practical AI demonstrated its potential to solve real-world problems.

The First Practical Applications of AI: One of the earliest applications of AI was in the field of game playing. In 1956, the first AI program, Logic Theorist, was developed by Allen Newell and Herbert A. Simon. This program was capable of proving mathematical theorems. Another significant early application was ELIZA, developed in the 1960s by Joseph Weizenbaum. ELIZA was an early natural language processing program that simulated conversation, demonstrating the potential of AI in human-computer interaction.

The Impact These Early Applications Had: These early AI systems, though limited in scope, provided valuable insights into the potential and challenges of AI. They also laid the groundwork for more advanced AI systems, sparking interestand investment in AI research. The success of these early applications showed that AI could be applied to solve specific, complex problems, leading to further development in fields like robotics, natural language processing, and expert systems.

1.6 The Rapid Development of Artificial Intelligence

The past few decades have seen an exponential growth in AI capabilities, driven by advancements in computing power, data availability, and algorithmic innovation.

Factors Contributing to the Rapid Advancement of AI: Several factors have contributed to the rapid development of AI. First, the dramatic increase in computing power, particularly with the advent of powerful GPUs, has enabled the processing of large datasets at unprecedented speeds. Second, the rise of big data has provided the raw material needed to train machine learning models effectively. Third, innovations in algorithms, particularly deep learning techniques, have significantly improved the accuracy and versatility of AI systems.

Examples of Recent AI Applications: Recent AI applications showcase its diverse capabilities. In health care , AI is being used to develop personalised treatment plans based on genetic data. In transportation, AI powers autonomous vehicles that cannavigate complex environments with minimal human intervention. In the creative industries, AI is being used to generate art, music, and even film scripts, pushing the boundaries of what machines can achieve. These examples highlight the transformative impact of AI across multiples rectors.

1.7 Future Predictions for Artificial Intelligence
As AI continues to evolve, it is poised to have even moreprofound effects on society. Understanding the potential future directions of AI helps in preparing for its broader implications.

Future Visions for AI Development: The future of AI is likely tosee the continued advancement of narrow AI systems, making them even more specialised and effective in their respective domains. There is also significant interest in developing GeneralAI, although this remains a long-term goal. Additionally, AI isexpected to become more integrated with other technologies, such as quantum computing and the Internet of Things (IoT), leading to new applications and possibilities.

Its Potential Impacts on Our Lives: The potential impacts of AI are vast. In the workplace, AI could lead to the automation of many jobs, requiring a shift in how societies think about employment and education. In health care, AI could revolutionise personalised medicine, leading to more effective treatments and possibly longer life spans. AI could also enhance our daily lives by creating smarter cities, improving energy efficiency, and enabling more effective communication. However, these advancements also raise ethical and societal questions that will need to be addressed as AI continues to develop.

This first chapter has provided a detailed exploration of the foundational aspects of Artificial Intelligence, setting the stage for a deeper dive into its applications, challenges, and potential in the following chapters. Understanding the history and evolution of AI, the key figures who have shaped its development, and the various forms it takes are crucial steps in appreciating the transformative power of this technology. As we move forward, we will explore how AI can be harnessed to achieve financial independence, among other significant outcomes.

Chapter 2: Artificial Intelligence in the Economy

Artificial Intelligence (AI) is reshaping economies across the globe, fundamentally altering how industries operate, how markets function, and how individuals engage with economic activities. This chapter delves into the profound impact of AI on both global and local economies, explores its applications in financial sectors and stock markets, and discusses its role in the digital economy. Additionally, it addresses the significant challenges AI poses to traditional jobs and offers insights intohow individuals can adapt to these changes.

2.1 The Role of AI in the Global Economy:

AI has become a driving force in the global economy, influencing everything from production processes to consumer behaviour. Its integration into various sectors has led to increased efficiency, cost savings, and the creation of new business models.

The Impact of AI on Global Markets: AI technologies are-accelerating globalisation by enabling faster, more efficient decision-making and streamlining international operations. For example, AI-powered supply chain management systems allow companies to predict and respond to demand fluctuations in real-time, reducing waste and improving profitability. Moreover, AI's ability to analyse vast amounts of data has enhanced the precision of market predictions, making global markets more interconnected and responsive to changes.

Examples of AI Use in Major Corporations: Major corporations like Google, Amazon, and IBM have heavily invested in AI to maintain their competitive edge. Google's AI algorithms, for instance, power its search engine, ad targeting, and even its self-driving car initiatives. Amazon uses AI for everything from recommendation engines to optimising its massive logistics network. IBM's Watson, a question-answering AI, is used in various industries, from health care to finance, to provide insights and make complex decisions. These corporations demonstrate how AI can be a critical asset in scaling operation sand staying ahead in competitive markets.

2.2 AI in Local Economic Sectors

While AI's influence on the global stage is significant, its impact on local economies is equally profound. AI is transforming local industries by optimizing processes, reducing costs, and enabling new forms of economic activity.

AI Applications in Local Industries: In agriculture, AI is used for precision farming, where drones and sensors collect data that helps farmers optimise water usage, predict crop yields, and reduce the use of fertilisers . In manufacturing, AI-driven robotics are increasingly used to perform repetitive tasks with high precision, reducing human error and production costs. Inretail, local businesses use AI to analyze consumer data andtailor their offerings to meet the specific needs of their customer base , enhancing customer satisfaction and loyalty.

Examples and Case Studies of Local Implementations: A case in point is the use of AI in local government services in Estonia, where AI systems are employed to automate public services, such as tax filing and legal document processing, improving efficiency and reducing the burden on civil servants. Another example is the implementation of AI in India's agriculture sector , where AI is used to provide farmers with timely weather forecasts and market prices, helping them make informed decisions and improve their income.

2.3 AI in Financial Sectors:

The financial sector is one of the most dynamic areas for AI application. From automating routine tasks to making complex financial predictions, AI is revolutionising how financial institutions operate and how individuals manage their wealth.

The Use of AI in Asset Management and Finance: AI is being used to enhance asset management through predictive analytics and machine learning algorithms that analyse market trends, economic indicators, and financial data to optimize investment strategies. Robo-advisors, which are AI-driven platforms, provide personalised financial advice and portfolio management, making financial planning more accessible to a broader audience. Additionally, AI helps financial institutions detect fraudulent activities by analysing transaction patterns and flagging suspicious behavior.

Examples of Intelligent Financial Systems: An example of AI infinance is JPMorgan Chase's COIN, an AI system that reviews legal documents and extracts relevant data in seconds, a task that used to take human lawyers thousands of hours. Similarly, BlackRock, the world's largest asset manager, uses AI to monitor global markets and make investment decisions based on real-time data. These systems not only improve efficiency but also reduce the risk of human error in critical financial decisions .

2.4 AI in Stock Markets:

Stock markets are highly dynamic environments where AI's ability to process vast amounts of data quickly gives it a significant advantage. AI is increasingly being used in trading and speculation, where speed and accuracy are critical.

AI Applications in Trading and Speculation: High-frequency trading (HFT) is one area where AI has a profound impact. HFT firms use AI algorithms to execute trades in fractions of a second, capitalizing on minute price discrepancies. These AI-driven strategies can analyse market data, news reports, and even social media sentiment to predict stock price movements and execute trades with minimal human intervention. Additionally, AI is used in algorithmic trading to develop strategies that maximise returns while minimizing risk.

Examples of Trading Algorithms: One not able example is renaissance Technologies' Medallion Fund, which uses AI-driven algorithms to analyze and trade in global markets, consistently outperforming the market with its data-driven approach. Another example is the use of AI by Goldman Sachs, where AI algorithms assist in making trading decisions by analysing vast datasets, including market trends, economic indicators, and even geopolitical events.

2.5 AI and Personal Investment:

AI is not just for large corporations and financial institutions; it also offers powerful tools for individual investors. By leveraging AI, individuals can make more informed investment decisions and potentially achieve financial independence.

How to Use AI to Improve Investment Decisions: Individuals can use AI-powered platforms like robo-advisors to get personalised investment advice based on their financial goals, risk tolerance, and market conditions. These platforms use machine learning algorithms to analyze vast amounts of financial data and suggest optimal investment strategies. Additionally, AI-driven apps can help investors monitor their portfolios in real-time, alerting them to opportunities or risks they might otherwise overlook.

Free Tools to Achieve Financial Independence: There are several AI-powered tools available for free or at a low cost that individuals can use to manage their investments. For example, apps like Wealth front and Betterment provide automated investment management, while platforms like Robinhood use AI to help users trade stocks without paying commissions. These tools empower individuals to take control of their financial futures with the same level of sophistication as professional investors.

2.6 AI and the Digital Economy:

The digital economy is rapidly expanding, and AI is at its core, driving innovation and enabling new business models that were previously unimaginable.

The Role of AI in the Development of the Digital Economy: AI technologies are the backbone of many digital platforms and services. For example, AI powers recommendation engines that drive engagement on platforms like Netflix and Spotify, ensuring users discover content that matches their preferences. In e-commerce, AI is used for dynamic pricing, inventory management, and customer service chatbots, enhancing the overall shopping experience and boosting sales.

Examples of Successful Digital Projects Enabled by AI: AI has enabled the creation of new digital services and products that have transformed industries. For example, Uber and Lyft use AI to optimize ride pricing and route planning, making transportation more efficient. In the health care industry, AI-driven telemedicine platforms provide patients with access to medical consultations without the need for in-person visits, expanding health care access. These examples highlight how AI is a key driver in the digital transformation of various sectors.

2.7 The Impact of AI on Traditional Jobs:

As AI continues to advance, it is disrupting traditional job markets, creating both challenges and opportunities for workers across various industries.

The Challenges AI Poses to the Job Market: AI's ability to automate routine and repetitive tasks poses a significant challenge to traditional jobs, particularly in manufacturing, customer service, and administrative roles. For example, AI-powered chatbots and customer service platforms are increasingly replacing human agents, while AI-driven robots are taking over assembly line tasks in manufacturing. This shift raises concerns about job displacement and the need for workers to acquire new skills to remain competitive in the job market.

How to Adapt to These Changes: To adapt to the changes brought by AI, workers need to focus on acquiring skills that areless susceptible to automation, such as creative problem-solving, critical thinking, and emotional intelligence. Continuous learning and ups killing are essential, as is the ability to work alongside AI systems in a collaborative manner. Educational institutions and governments also have a role to play inpreparing the workforce for the AI-driven economy by providing access to training programs and resources.

Conclusion

AI's impact on the economy is far-reaching, influencing global markets, local industries, financial sectors, and even individual investment strategies. While it brings numerous opportunities for innovation and efficiency, it also presents challenges, particularly in the job market. As AI continues to evolve, its rolein the economy will only grow, making it essential for businesses and individuals alike to understand and adapt to these changes to thrive in the AI-driven world.

Chapter 3: Artificial Intelligence in Security and Defense

Artificial Intelligence (AI) has emerged as a transformative force in the fields of security and defense, revolutionising how nations safeguard their borders, protect critical infrastructure, and engage in military operations. This chapter delves into the diverse applications of AI in national security, military defense, intelligence gathering, infrastructure protection, counterterrorism, and international cooperation. It also addresses the ethical challenges associated with deploying AI in these sensitive areas, exploring the implications for global security and governance.

3.1 AI in National Security:

AI plays an increasingly vital role in enhancing national security by providing tools that enable governments to monitor, detect, and respond to threats more effectively.

The Role of AI in Enhancing Internal Security: AI systems are being integrated into national security frame works to help identify and mitigate internal threats, such as criminal activities, cyber-attacks, and civil unrest. Through the use of machine learning algorithms, AI can analyze vast amounts of data from various sources, including social media, CCTV footage, and public records, to detect patterns that might indicate potential security breaches. These systems can also predict incidents based on historical data and real-time information, allowing security agencies to preemptively address issues before they escalate.

Examples of AI-Based Security Systems: One example is theuse of facial recognition technology in public surveillance systems, which helps law enforcement agencies identify suspects and track their movements across cities. Another is predictive policing, where AI algorithms analyse crime data to predict where crimes are likely to occur, enabling law enforcement to allocate resources more efficiently. In cybersecurity , AI-powered systems like Fire Eye and Dark trace monitor network traffic for anomalies, identifying and responding to potential cyber threats in real-time.

3.2 AI in Military Defence:

In the realm of military defence, AI is transforming the development and deployment of advanced weapons systems, enhancing the strategic capabilities of armed forces around the world.

AI Applications in Military Equipment and Systems: AI is being integrated into various aspects of military operations, from autonomous vehicles to advanced weapons systems. AI enables these systems to process information, make decisions, and carry out tasks with minimal human intervention, increasing the speed and effectiveness of military responses. AI-driven systems canalso analyse battlefield data in real-time, providing commanders with actionable insights that can influence the outcome of engagements.

Examples of Drones and Military Robots: AI-powered drone's have become a staple in modern war fare, used for surveillance, reconnaissance, and even targeted strikes. For instance, the U.S. military's MQ-9 Reaper drone uses AI to process vast amounts of data, identify targets, and execute precision strikes with minimal human input. Similarly, military robots like theMAARS (Modular Advanced Armed Robotic System) are equipped with AI to navigate complex environments, engage threats, and perform tasks such as bomb disposal, reducing the risk to human soldiers.

3.3 AI in Intelligence Gathering:

AI is revolutionising intelligence gathering by enabling the analysis of massive data sets that would be impossible for human analysts to process manually.

AI Applications in Intelligence Data Collection: AI systems are being used to collect and analyse data from a wide array of sources, including satellite imagery, intercepted communications, and social media. These systems use natural language processing, image recognition, and machine learning algorithms to sift through this data, identifying relevant information that could indicate potential threats or valuable intelligence.

Examples of Smart Systems for Security Analysis : Palantir, a data analytics company, has developed AI systems that are usedby intelligence agencies to analyse vast datasets and identify patterns that might suggest terrorist activity or other security threats. Another example is Project Maven, an initiative by theU.S. Department of Defence that uses AI to analyse video footage captured by drones, helping to identify potential targetsmore quickly and accurately.

3.4 Protecting Critical Infrastructure with AI:

AI plays a crucial role in safeguarding critical infrastructure, such as energy grids, communication networks, and transportation systems, from both physical and cyber threats.

The Role of AI in Safeguarding Energy and Communication Infrastructures: AI systems are being deployed to monitor and protect vital infrastructure against disruptions. These systems can detect anomalies in network traffic, monitor for potential intrusions, and even predict failures in critical systems before they occur. By analysing data in real-time, AI can help ensure the stability and security of infrastructure that is essential for national security and economic stability.

Examples of Systems Protecting Critical Infrastructure: The use of AI in protecting power grids is a prime example. AI algorithms can predict equipment failures based on patterns in-sensor data, enabling preventive maintenance and reducing the risk of outages. Similarly, in communication networks, AI can detect and respond to cyber-attacks, preventing the disruption of services. Companies like Siemens and IBM are developing AI-driven systems that monitor industrial control systems and protect them from both physical and cyber threats.

3.5 Combating Terrorism with AI:

AI is becoming an essential tool in the fight against terrorism, helping to identify and neutralise threats before they can materialise.

How AI Helps in Identifying Terrorist Threats: AI systems can analyse data from various sources, such as online communications, financial transactions, and travel records, to identify individuals who may pose a terrorist threat. Thesesystems can detect patterns of behavior that are consistent with known terrorist activities, helping security agencies to intervene before an attack occurs. AI can also be used to monitor social media and other online platforms for extremist content, providing early warnings of potential radicalisation.

Examples of AI Programs Used in Counterterrorism: One notable example is the use of AI by the European Union'sINDECT project, which combines data from various sources to detect abnormal behaviors that could indicate terrorist activities. In the United States, the FBI uses AI tools to analyse vast amounts of data from various sources, helping to identify and track individuals involved in terrorist networks. AI is also used in border security to screen travelers and identify those who may-pose a threat.

3.6 AI and International Cooperation in Security:

As AI becomes more integral to security and defence, international cooperation is essential to address common threat sand establish norms for the use of AI in military and security contexts.

International Collaboration in AI for Security Purposes: Countries around the world are recognising the need for international cooperation in the development and deployment of AI for security purposes. This collaboration includes sharing intelligence, developing common standards for AI use insecurity, and coordinating responses to global threats. Such cooperation is vital for ensuring that AI is used responsibly and effectively in maintaining international security.

Examples of International Initiatives: The NATO CooperativeCyber Defence Centre of Excellence (CCDCOE) is one example-of international collaboration on AI in security. This center brings together experts from various countries to develop strategies for using AI in cyber security and other aspects of national defence. Another example is the Global Partnership onAI (GPAI), an international initiative that includes efforts to-ensure the ethical and effective use of AI in security and defence.

3.7 Ethical Challenges of Using AI in Security and Defence:

While AI offers significant advantages in security and defence, its use raises important ethical questions that must be addressed to prevent misuse and ensure compliance with international laws.

Discussion of Ethical Issues Related to AI Use in Security: The use of AI in security and defence raises several ethical concerns, including issues of accountability, transparency, and the potential for bias in AI systems. There are also concerns about the use of autonomous weapons systems, which could make life-and-death decisions without human intervention. The potential for AI to be used in ways that violate human rights, such as mass surveillance or targeted assassinations, also presents significant ethical challenges.

Case Studies and International Stances: One prominent case study is the controversy surrounding the use of autonomous drones in military operations. Critics argue that these systems lack the human judgment necessary to make ethical decisions in complex combat situations. Internationally, there is a growing movement to establish norms and regulations for the use of AI in warfare, with organisations like the United Nations calling for a ban on autonomous weapons systems. The European Union has also taken a strong stance on the ethical use of AI, emphasising the need for transparency, accountability, and respect for human rights in the development and deployment of AI systems.

Conclusion:

AI is rapidly transforming the fields of security and defense, offering powerful tools for protecting national interests and responding to global threats. However, the integration of AI into these areas also presents significant challenges, particularly interms of ethics and international cooperation. As AI continues to-evolve, it is crucial for governments, organizations, and societies to navigate these challenges carefully, ensuring that AI is used in ways that enhance security while respecting humanrights and international law.

Chapter 4: Artificial Intelligence in Everyday Life:

Artificial intelligence has permeated every aspect of our daily lives, fundamentally changing how we interact with technology, receive services, and engage in various activities. This chapter delves into the various applications of AI in everyday life, from transportation and home services to health care , education, social media , entertainment, and shopping. By understanding these applications , we can appreciate the transformative impact of AI on our daily routines and anticipate future developments that will continue to shape our world.

4.1 AI in Transportation:

Transportation is one of the most visible and rapidly evolving areas of AI application. The integration of AI in transportation systems is not only transforming how we travel but also how goods are delivered, and how cities manage traffic and safety. Self-driving cars and smart transportation applications: Self-driving cars are perhaps the most iconic example of AI in transportation. These vehicles use a combination of machine learning algorithms, computer vision, and sensor data to navigate roads, interpret traffic signals, avoid obstacles, and make real-time decisions, all without human intervention. AI enables these cars to learn from vast amounts of driving data, continuously improving their safety and efficiency. Besides self-driving cars, AI is also used in smart transportation systems, which optimize traffic flow, reduce congestion, and enhance public transportation services. AI-powered traffic management systems can predict traffic patterns and adjust signals accordingly to minimise delays.

Examples of leading companies in this field: Several companies are at the fore front of AI-driven transportation innovations. Tesla, for example, has integrated AI into its vehicles to provide advanced driver-assistance systems (ADAS) and autopilot features . Waymo, a subsidiary of Alphabet Inc., has developed fully autonomous vehicles that are being tested on public roads. Uber and Lyft are also investing in AI to develop self-driving taxis, while traditional automotive giants like Ford and GeneralMotors are collaborating with tech companies to integrate AI into their vehicles.

4.2 AI in Home Services

AI has found its way into our homes, making daily chores easier and enhancing our living environments. Through smart devices and home robots, AI is reshaping domestic life by providing convenience, efficiency, and improved quality of life.

Home robots and smart assistants: Home robots equipped with AI are becoming increasingly common, performing tasks such as vacuuming, lawn mowing, and even cooking.

These robots use AI to navigate spaces, recognise objects, and carry out specific tasks autonomously. Mean while, smart assistants like Amazon's Alexa, Google Assistant, and Apple's Siri use natural language processing and machine learning to understand and respond to voice commands, control smart home devices, manage schedules, and provide information. These AI systems learn from user interactions to improve their responses and adapt to individual preferences.

Examples of smart home devices: The market is flooded withAI-powered smart home devices that simplify daily routines. Smart thermostats like Nest learn user habits to optimise heating and cooling systems, reducing energy consumption and costs. AI-enabled security systems, such as Ring, use facial recognition and motion detection to monitor homes and alert homeowners of potential security threats. Smart refrigerators can track food inventory, suggest recipes, and even order groceries when supplies are low. These devices not only offer convenience but also contribute to a more efficient and sustainable life style.

4.3 AI in Healthcare:

The healthcare industry is experiencing a revolution with the integration of AI, which is enhancing the accuracy of diagnoses, the efficiency of treatments, and the overall quality of care.

The use of AI in diagnosis and treatment: AI is being used to analyse medical data, identify patterns, and assist in diagnosing conditions that may be difficult for human clinicians to detect. Machine learning algorithms can process imaging data fromMRIs, CT scans, and X-rays, detecting anomalies that could indicate diseases such as cancer at an earlier stage than possible with traditional methods. In treatment, AI is being used to personalise medicine, developing treatment plans tailored to individual patients based on their genetic information, medical history, and lifestyle. AI-powered robots are also being used insurgery, providing precision that enhances patient outcomes.

Examples of AI tools in hospitals* AI tools like IBM Watson forOncology assist doctors by providing evidence-based treatment options for cancer patients, drawing from vast medical literature. The AI platform DeepMind, owned by Google, has developed systems to predict patient deterioration in hospitals, enabling timely interventions. AI-driven chatbots are being used in telemedicine to assess symptoms and provide preliminary diagnoses, reducing the burden on healthcare professionals and improving access to care.

4.4 AI in Education:

Education is another area where AI is making significant strides, offering new ways to personalise learning, improve educational outcomes, and make education more accessible. AI applications in enhancing education: AI is being used to create personalised learning experiences that cater to the individual needs of students. Adaptive learning platforms use AI to analyse students' performance, identify strengths and weaknesses, and adjust content and pacing accordingly. This approach helps students learn at their own pace, ensuring they master foundational concepts before moving on to more advanced material. AI is also being used to automate administrative tasks, such as grading and scheduling, freeing upeducators to focus more on teaching and student interaction. Examples of smart learning systems: Smart learning systems like Coursera and Khan Academy utilise AI to recommend courses and resources tailored to learners' interests and needs. EdTech companies such as DreamBox and ALEKS use AI to-offer personalised math instruction, adapting to students' learning styles and knowledge levels. Language learning platforms like Duolingo employ AI to create customised lessons that respond to how well users are learning and retaining information.

4.5 AI in Social Media:

AI plays a crucial role in how we interact on social media platforms, influencing what content we see, how we communicate , and how these platforms manage user behavior. How AI changes our interaction on social media platforms: Social media platforms use AI algorithms to curate content, ensuring that users are shown posts, videos, and ads that are most likely to engage them. These algorithms analyse user behaviour, such as likes, shares, comments, and time spent on specific content, to tailor the feed accordingly. AI is also used to moderate content, automatically detecting and removing inappropriate or harmful posts based on predefined criteria. This technology helps platforms manage vast amounts of content while maintaining a safe environment for users. Examples of systems that analyse and guide social content: Facebook uses AI to prioritise content in users' news feeds, while Twitter's AI systems recommend tweets and users to follow based on interests and interactions. LinkedIn leveragesAI to suggest job opportunities and professional connections, enhancing networking and career growth. Additionally, AI isemployed to combat misinformation and fake news, with platforms like YouTube and Instagram using machine learning to identify and reduce the spread of false information.

4.6 AI in Entertainment and Arts:

The entertainment and arts industries are experiencing a renaissance driven by AI, with new forms of creative expression emerging alongside traditional media.

AI applications in music and film production: AI is transforming music production by composing original scores, suggesting melodies, and even mixing tracks. AI tools like Amper Musicand AIVA can generate music tailored to specific moods orthemes, assisting composers and producers in the creative process. In film production, AI is used to analyse scripts, predict box office success, and even edit footage. AI-driven animationand visual effects are creating more realistic and immersive experiences, as seen in movies like "The Lion King" (2019), which used AI to enhance its photorealistic animation.

Examples of artistic works created by AI: AI is increasingly being recognized as a creative force in its own right. For example, the AI program "DeepDream" by Google has been used to create surreal, dream-like images that have been exhibited in art galleries. In 2018, a painting titled "Portrait of Edmond de Belamy," created by the AI algorithm GAN (Generative Adversarial Network), was sold at Christie's auction house for $432,500, highlighting the growing acceptance of AI in the art world. AI is also being used in literature, with programs like OpenAI's GPT models generating poetry, stories, and even assisting in novel writing.

4.7 AI in Shopping and E-commerce:

The shopping experience has been revolutionised by AI, making it more personalised, efficient, and enjoyable for consumers.

How AI is used to improve the shopping experience: AI is employed in e-commerce to provide personalised recommendations , optimise pricing, and enhance customer service. By analysing user data such as purchase history, browsing behavior, and preferences, AI systems can suggest products that are most likely to appeal to individual shoppers. AI is also used in dynamic pricing, adjusting prices in real-time based on demand, competition, and other factors. In customer-service, AI-powered chatbots handle inquiries, assist with purchases, and resolve issues, providing instant support and improving the overall shopping experience.

Examples of websites and apps relying on AI: E-commerce giants like Amazon and Alibaba extensively use AI to personalise shopping experiences, recommend products, and optimise logistics.

Amazon's AI-driven recommendation engine is responsible for a significant portion of its sales, as it suggests products that users are likely to buy based on their behavior. Shopify, an e-commerce platform, uses AI to help merchants analyse customer data, manage inventory, and automate marketing campaigns. Apps like Stitch Fix use AI to offer personalised fashion recommendations, combining data-driven insights with human expertise to curate items tailored to individual tastes.

Conclusion:
Artificial intelligence is seamlessly integrating into everyday life, influencing how we travel, communicate, learn, and even entertain our selves. As AI continues to evolve, its role in our daily routines will only become more significant, offering new-opportunities and challenges. By understanding these applications, we can better navigate the rapidly changing technological landscape and harness AI's potential to improveour lives.

Chapter 5: AI and Financial Independence

5.1 How AI Can Achieve Financial Independence?
Strategies for Using AI to Generate Income:
AI offers numerous pathways to achieve financial independence by creating and managing income streams. Here are key strategies:
Automated Trading Systems: AI-driven trading platforms can analyze market trends and execute trades faster than human traders. By leveraging algorithms, investors can automate trading strategies, potentially increasing returns with minimal human intervention.

Content Creation: AI tools can assist in generating content, suchas blog posts, social media updates, and even creative works like music and art. This content can be monetised through advertising, sponsor ships, or direct sales.

Affiliate Marketing: AI can optimise affiliate marketing by analysing consumer behavior and suggesting targeted productsor services. This targeted approach can enhance conversion ratesand, consequently, income.

Examples of Success Stories:

Jasper (formerly Jarvis): An AI writing assistant that helps users create content quickly. Many bloggers and marketers have used Jasper to streamline their content creation processes and increase their earnings through more frequent and higher-quality outputs.

Etsy Sellers: Some Etsy sellers use AI tools to analyse market trends and optimise product listings, resulting in increased sales and a more substantial income.

5.2 AI Tools for Generating Passive Income

Applications and Systems:

Passive income through AI involves tools and systems that work autonomously, generating revenue with minimal ongoing effort. Key examples include:

AI-Driven Investment Platforms: Tools like Betterment or wealth front use AI to manage investment portfolios, automatically adjusting strategies based on market conditions to maximise returns.

Automated Dropshipping: Platforms like Oberlo or Sprocket integrate AI to manage inventory, process orders, and optimise pricing strategies for dropshipping businesses, allowing entrepreneurs to earn income with minimal day-to-day involvement.

Examples of Free and Paid Tools:

Free Tools: Google's AI-powered AdSense can help monetise website traffic through targeted ads. Additionally, AI-based email marketing platforms often offer free tiers with limited features.

Paid Tools: HubSpot's AI tools for content marketing and lead generation can significantly boost sales and require a subscription. Similarly, premium AI writing tools like write sonic offer advanced features for creating content.

5.3 AI in E-Commerce:

How to Benefit from AI in Online Selling: AI can revolutionise e-commerce by optimising various aspects of the business:

Personalisation: AI algorithms analyse customer data to offer personalised recommendations, increasing the likelihood of sales . For example, AI can suggest products based on previous browsing and purchase history.

Customer Service: Chatbots powered by AI provide 24/7 customer support, handling queries and issues efficiently. This improves customer satisfaction and can lead to higher retention rates.

Examples of Smart E-Commerce Tools: Shopify's AI Features: Shopify uses AI to provide insights into sales trends, customer behavior, and inventory management, helping merchants make data-driven decisions.

Dynamic Yield: An AI platform that offers personalised product recommendations and targeted marketing campaigns to enhance the shopping experience and drive sales.

5.4 AI and Remote Work:

How AI Facilitates Remote Work:
AI enhances remote work by streamlining communication, collaboration, and productivity:

Virtual Assistants: AI-powered virtual assistants help manage schedules, set reminders, and automate repetitive tasks, allowing remote workers to focus on higher-value activities.

Collaboration Tools: AI tools facilitate real-time translation, automated meeting summaries, and project management, making remote collaboration smoother and more efficient.

Examples of Companies Relying on AI for Remote Operations:

Slack: Uses AI for automated message categorisation, smart replies, and integration with other productivity tools, supporting effective remote team communication.

Asana: Employs AI to prioritise tasks, track project progress, and provide insights into team performance, aiding remote project management.

5.5 Investing in Artificial Intelligence

How to Invest in AI Companies: Investing in AI involves purchasing shares of companies that develop or utilise AI technology. Key considerations include:

Tech Giants: Investing in established companies like Google, Microsoft, and Amazon, which heavily invest in AI research and development, can be a way to gain exposure to AI advancements.

AI Startups: Investing in emerging AI startups through venture capital or equity crowdfunding platforms can offer high returns, though with greater risk.

Examples of Successful AI Startups:

OpenAI: Known for developing advanced AI models like GPT, OpenAI represents a high-profile example of innovative AI technology.

UiPath: Specialises in robotic process automation (RPA) and has gained significant traction in automating repetitive tasks across various industries.

5.6 AI and Time Management

Using AI Applications to Improve Personal Productivity:

AI applications can optimise personal time management by automating scheduling, task prioritisation, and reminders:

AI Scheduling Assistants: Tools like Clara or x.ai manage meeting schedules and send reminders, reducing the time spent on administrative tasks.

Task Management: AI-driven apps analyse user behavior to suggest the most efficient task schedules and prioritise important tasks, enhancing productivity.

Examples of Apps that Help Organize Time:

Todo its: Uses AI to prioritise tasks and provide productivity insights, helping users stay organized and focused.

Time Doctor: AI-based time tracking and productivity analysis tool that helps users understand how their time is spent and identify areas for improvement.

5.7 AI and Personal Marketing:

How AI Can Help Build Personal Branding:
AI tools assist in crafting and maintaining a personal brand by optimising content creation, audience engagement, and brand visibility:

Content Optimisation: AI tools analyze audience preferences and suggest content topics, formats, and posting schedules that resonate with target audiences.

Social Media Management: AI platforms can automate social media posting, analyze engagement metrics, and suggest strategies for improving online presence.

Examples of Tools That Make Self-Marketing Easier:

Buffer: An AI-driven social media management tool that schedules posts, tracks performance, and suggests engagement strategies.

Canva: Uses AI to offer design suggestions and templates, enabling users to create professional marketing materials without advanced design skills.

This chapter outlines various ways AI can be leveraged to achieve financial independence, enhance e-commerce operations, support remote work, facilitate investment, improve time management, and bolster personal marketing. By understanding and utilizing these AI applications and tools, individuals can optimize their income generation andproductivity efforts.

Chapter 6: AI and Society

6.1 The Impact of AI on the Job Market
Changes in the Job Market Due to AI:
AI is profoundly transforming the job market through automation, new job creation, and changes in required skills:
Automation of Routine Tasks: AI systems are increasingly capable of performing repetitive and routine tasks, such as data entry, customer service inquiries, and even complex processes like legal document analysis. This leads to job displacement in certain sectors but also shifts focus towards roles that involve more complex problem-solving and creative tasks.
Creation of New Job Categories: As AI technologies evolve, new job roles are emerging, including AI specialists, data scientists, machine learning engineers, and AI ethics consultants. These roles require a blend of technical skills and domain knowledge, reflecting the growing importance of AI invarious industries.

Shift in Skill Requirements: The demand for skills related to AI, such as programming, data analysis, and machine learning, is increasing. Conversely, skills in manual or repetitive tasks are becoming less relevant. Workers need to adapt by acquiring new-skills that align with the AI-driven economy.

How to Adapt to These Changes:

Adapting to the changes brought by AI involves several strategies:

Continuous Learning: Embrace life long learning to stay updated with the latest technological advancements and acquire new-skills relevant to AI. Online courses, certifications, and workshops can provide valuable knowledge and skills.

Career Flexibility:Be open to transitioning into roles that areless likely to be automated. Roles involving human creativity, complex problem-solving, and emotional intelligence are more resilient to automation.

Collaboration with AI: Learn how to work alongside AI systems effectively. Understanding how to use AI tools to enhance productivity and decision-making can provide a competitive edge in the evolving job market.

6.2 AI in Education:

How AI Contributes to Improving Education Quality:

AI enhances education by personalising learning experiences, automating administrative tasks, and providing data-driven insights:

Personalised Learning: AI systems can analyse student performance and learning styles to tailor educational content and teaching methods. This individualised approach helps address diverse learning needs and improves student outcomes.

Automated Administrative Tasks: AI can automate tasks such as grading, scheduling, and managing student records, allowing educators to focus more on teaching and less on administrative work.

Data-Driven Insights: AI tools analyse educational data to identify trends, predict student performance, and suggest interventions. This helps educators make informed decisions to enhance teaching strategies and support student success.

Data-Driven Insights: AI tools analyse educational data to identify trends, predict student performance, and suggest interventions. This helps educators make informed decisions to enhance teaching strategies and support student success.

Examples of Smart Educational Initiatives:
Khan Academy's AI-Powered Tools: Khan Academy uses AI to-offer personalised learning experiences and adaptive practice exercises based on student performance and needs.

Duolingo: An AI-driven language learning app that adapts to individual learning paces and styles, providing tailored exercises and feedback to enhance language acquisition.

6.3 AI in Public Services:

The Role of AI in Improving Government Services:

AI enhances public services by increasing efficiency, accuracy, and accessibility:

Efficient Service Delivery: AI-powered chatbots and virtual assistants streamline interactions with government agencies, providing quick responses to common queries and reducing waittimes.

Predictive Analytics: AI systems analyse data to predict and address public issues, such as crime patterns, traffic congestion, and health care needs, allowing for proactive and informed policy decisions.

Fraud Detection: AI algorithms identify patterns indicative of fraudulent activities, enhancing the integrity of public services and reducing financial losses.

Examples of AI Applications in the Public Sector:

Singapore's Smart Nation Initiative: Uses AI to improve urban planning, manage traffic, and enhance public safety through data analysis and predictive modeling.

Los Angeles' Predictive Policing Program: Employs AI to analyse crime data and predict potential crime hotspots, allowing for more effective resource allocation and crime prevention strategies.

6.4 AI in Medicine and Healthcare:

How AI is Changing the Future of Healthcare:

AI is revolutionising healthcare by improving diagnostics, treatment, and patient care:

Enhanced Diagnostics: AI algorithms analyse medical image sand patient data to detect diseases with high accuracy, such ascancer, cardiovascular conditions, and neurological disorders, often surpassing human capabilities.

Personalised Treatment: AI systems use patient data to recommend personalised treatment plans, optimising drug-dosages and predicting responses to treatments, there by improving patient outcomes.

Operational Efficiency: AI helps streamline administrative tasks, manage patient records, and optimise hospital operations, leading to cost reductions and improved healthcare delivery.

Examples of Medical AI Applications:

IBM Watson Health: Uses AI to analyze vast amounts of medical data to assist in diagnosing diseases and recommending treatment options.

DeepMind's AI for Eye Health: An AI system developed by DeepMind that analyses retinal scans to detect signs of eye diseases and conditions at an early stage.

6.5 AI and the Environment

Using AI to Improve Natural Resource Management:

AI contributes to environmental sustainability by optimising resource use, monitoring ecosystems, and predicting environmental changes:

Resource Management: AI systems help manage natural resources more efficiently by analysing data on consumption patterns, predicting future needs, and optimising resource allocation.

Ecosystem Monitoring: AI tools analyse satellite images and sensor data to monitor environmental changes, track wildlife populations, and assess the health of ecosystems.

Examples of Applications in Agriculture and Energy:

Precision Agriculture: AI-driven technologies like drones and sensors monitor crop health, optimise irrigation, and predict harvest times, enhancing agricultural productivity and sustainability.

Smart Grids: AI helps manage energy distribution in smart grids, balancing supply and demand, integrating renewable energy sources, and improving energy efficiency.

6.6 AI in Humanitarian Aid:
The Role of AI in Enhancing Crisis Response:
AI improves humanitarians aid by providing faster, more accurate responses to crises and optimising resource distribution:
Data Analysis for Prioritisation: AI analyses data from various sources to assess needs, prioritise aid distribution, and coordinate response efforts, ensuring that resources reach those in most need.
Predictive Analytics for Crisis Management: AI models predict the impact of natural disasters, disease out breaks, and other emergencies, enabling preemptive measures and efficient resource allocation.
Examples of AI Projects that Have Provided Rapid and effective Humanitarian Aid:

Crisis Text Line: Uses AI to analyse text messages and identify individuals in urgent need of support, enabling timely intervention and assistance.

The World Food Programme's AI Solutions: Employs AI to optimise food distribution logistics, predict food shortages, and manage supply chains in crisis-affected areas.

6.7 AI and Humanitarian Assistance:

The Role of AI in Crisis Response:

AI enhances crisis response by analysing data to prioritise and streamline humanitarian efforts:

Data Analysis for Prioritisation: AI algorithms analyse real-time data from social media, satellite imagery, and other sources to identify affected areas and prioritise aid distribution based on urgency.

Examples of AI Projects: AI systems used by organisations like the UN and Red Cross to assess disaster impacts, coordinate relief efforts, and allocate resources efficiently.

Big Data Analysis in Disaster Management:

AI improves disaster planning and response through the analysis of large datasets:

Disaster Prediction: AI models predict the occurrence and impact of natural disasters, such as hurricanes and earthquakes, based on historical data and real-time information.
Examples of Systems: AI tools like the Pacific Disaster Center'searly warning systems use big data to forecast disasters and guide emergency responses.
Smart Applications in Humanitarian Relief:
AI applications ensure fair distribution of aid and resources incrisis situations:
Fair Distribution:AI systems track and manage resource allocation, ensuring that aid reaches all affected individuals equitably.
Examples of Tools:AI platforms used by NGOs to monitor and coordinate relief operations, track supplies, and manage logistics .
Technology and Privacy in Humanitarian Work:
AI usage in humanitarian work raises privacy and ethical concerns:
Privacy Challenges:The collection and analysis of personal datafor aid purposes can lead to privacy issues and misuse of information.
Case Studies:Instances where AI applications have faced criticism for data handling practices and ethical dilemmas, highlighting the need for robust privacy safeguards.
AI and International Cooperation in Crises:

AI fosters international cooperation in managing crises:
Enhanced Cooperation: AI tools facilitate collaboration between countries and humanitarian organisations by sharing data, coordinating responses, and integrating efforts.
Examples of Joint Projects: Collaborative projects such as the Global Disaster Alert and Coordination System (GDACS) use AI to enhance international crisis management.
AI Applications in Reconstruction:
AI plays a role in rebuilding communities after disasters:
Reconstruction Efforts: AI supports reconstruction by analysing damage, planning rebuilding strategies, and optimising resource allocation.
Examples of Initiatives: AI-driven projects that assist in assessing damage, planning infrastructure repairs, and managing reconstruction efforts in disaster-stricken areas.
The Future of AI in Humanitarian Work:
AI's future role in humanitarian efforts includes:
Future Outlook: Continued advancements in AI are expected to enhance crisis response, resource management, and aid distribution.
New Technologies: Emerging technologies such as advanced machine learning models and robotics may further improve humanitarian aid and disaster response.
This chapter explores how AI impacts various societal domains, including the job market, education, public services, healthcare, environmental management, humanitarian aid, and international cooperation . By understanding these applications and their implications , we can better appreciate the transformative role of AI in addressing societal challenges and advancing global well-being.

Chapter 7: AI in Cultural and Artistic Fields

7.1 AI in Music:
Analysing Musical Patterns:
AI enhances the understanding of music through pattern recognition and analysis:
Pattern Recognition:AI algorithms can analyse complex musical compositions to identify patterns in rhythm, harmony, melody, and structure. By processing vast amounts of musical data, AI can uncover patterns that might be difficult for human analysts-to discern.
Artificial Music Generation Systems:AI systems, such asOpenAI's MuseNet and Google's Magenta, generate music by learning from existing compositions. These systems use deep learning models to compose original pieces or mimic the styles of various composers, often producing music that is both innovative and stylistically consistent.

Creating Music with AI:
AI has transformed music composition by enabling automated creation :
AI Composing Tools: Tools like Amper Music and AIVA (Artificial Intelligence Virtual Artist) use algorithms to compose music based on user inputs or predefined styles. These systems generate melodies, harmonies, and rhythms, allowing for the creation of new musical pieces without direct human intervention .
Examples of AI-Created Music: In 2019, AIVA's composition was performed by a live orchestra, show casing how AI can produce complete musical works. Similarly, the album "I AM AI" by Taryn Southern was composed using AI, demonstrating the potential for AI to contribute significantly to music creation.
Enhancing Music Production with AI:
AI enhances various aspects of music production, improving quality and efficiency:
Quality Improvement:AI-driven tools can automate mixing and mastering processes, optimizing sound quality. For instance, LANDR offers AI-powered mastering services that analyse and enhance tracks based on genre-specific standards.
Tools and Software:AI tools like iZotope's Ozone and Soon suite leverage machine learning to assist musicians in achieving professional-grade sound. These tools provide features like intelligent EQ adjustments, noise reduction, and automated remixing.

7.2 AI in Visual Arts:

Generating Digital Art:

AI is increasingly used to create visually compelling artwork:

AI Art Generation: Algorithms such as Generative Adversarial Networks (GANs) generate new images based on learned data from existing artworks. GANs can create pieces that emulate different artistic styles or produce entirely novel art forms.

Examples: The artist and researcher Mario Klingemann uses AI to create abstract and surreal artworks. Another example is the portrait "Edmond de Belamy," created by the Paris-based collective Obvious using a GAN, which sold at auction for $432,500 in 2018.

Human-Machine Interaction in Arts:

The collaboration between humans and AI in art production:

Artist-AI Collaboration: Artists use AI as a tool to explore new creative possibilities. For instance, artist Refik Anadol employs AI to create immersive digital installations that blend art with data visualisation.

Collaborative Projects: Projects like "The Next Rembrandt," where AI was used to generate a new painting in the style of Rembrandt, highlight the potential for AI-human collaboration in art. This project involved analysing Rembrandt's works and creating a new piece that mimicked his style.

7.3 AI in Cinema:

Film Production with AI:

AI contributes to various stages of film production:

Editing and Production: AI tools assist in video editing by automating tasks such as scene recognition, color correction, and sound editing. For example, Adobe's Sensei uses AI to enhance video content creation by offering features like automatic scene detection and smart cropping.

Examples: Films such as "Zone Out," directed by Andrew "Moj" McLuhan, used AI for scene analysis and editing. AI-powered tools also help in script writing by suggesting plot developments and character dialogues based on analysis of successful scripts.

Analysing Scripts and Actors' Performances:

AI improves script writing and performance analysis:

Script Analysis: AI tools like Script AI analyse script elements such as dialogue, plot structure, and character development to suggest improvements or predict a script's success.

Performance Evaluation: AI-driven software can analyze actors' performances by assessing facial expressions, voice modulation, and body language to provide feedback and guide actors in their roles.

7.4 AI in Literature and Publishing

Creating Literary Texts:

AI aids in generating written content, from stories to novels:

AI in Writing Tools like GPT-3 by OpenAI and NovelAI can generate coherent and contextually relevant text based on user inputs. These systems are used for drafting stories, creating dialogue, and even completing novels.

Examples: The book "1 the Road," co-written by AI and author Ross Goodwin, is an example of AI's role in literature. The AI generated text based on input from a road trip, creating a unique narrative.

Analysing Literary Texts:

AI helps in the analysis and interpretation of literary works:

Text Analysis: AI tools such as Voyant Tools and Literary Hub's AI use natural language processing to analyse themes, sentiment, and stylistic elements in literature. This helps scholars and readers gain deeper insights into texts.

Interpretation Tools: AI-driven platforms can identify patterns in literary genres, track the evolution of literary styles, and offer comparative analyses of classical and modern works.

7.5 AI in Digital Games:

Developing Games with AI:

AI plays a significant role in the development of video games:

Game Development: AI is used to create more dynamic and interactive game environments. Procedural generation algorithms create complex game worlds, while AI-driven non-player characters (NPCs) offer realistic behaviors and responses.

Examples: Games like "No Man's Sky" use procedural generation to create vast, explorable universes, while "Left 4 Dead" employs AI to dynamically adjust the difficulty level based on player performance.

Personalizing the Gaming Experience:

AI enhances player experiences by adapting to individual preferences:

Customisation: AI algorithms analyse player behavior to personalise game experiences, such as adjusting difficulty levels, recommending in-game items, or tailoring narratives based on player choices.

Examples: The game "Middle-earth: Shadow of Mordor" features an AI system called the Nemesis System, which personalises interactions with enemies based on player actionsand decisions.

7.6 AI in Media and Publishing:

Generating Media Content:

AI contributes to the creation of news and media content:

Content Creation: AI systems generate news reports, articles, and other media content by analysing data and identifying key trends. For example, the Associated Press uses AI to automate the writing of financial reports and sports summaries.

Examples: Platforms like Wordsmith by Automated Insights create data-driven reports and articles. This technology allows news organisations to produce high volumes of content efficiently.

Analysing Audience Reactions:

AI aids in understanding and optimizing audience engagement:

Audience Analysis: AI tools analyse social media feedback, viewer metrics, and engagement data to provide insights into audience preferences and reactions. This helps media companies tailor content and improve strategies.

Examples: Tools like Crimson Hexagon and Brand watch use AI to analyze social media sentiment and trends, helping publishers and media outlets understand audience opinions and refine content strategies.

7.7 AI in Literary and Artistic Translation

Improving the Quality of Literary Translation: AI enhances the translation of literary and artistic texts:

Advanced Translation Systems: AI-driven translation tools, suchas Google Translate and DeepL, use neural networks to provide more accurate and contextually appropriate translations of literary texts.

Examples: Projects like the Google Books Library utilise AI to translate and digitise classic literature, making these works accessible to a global audience in multiple languages.

Reviving Classical Literary Works:

AI helps modernise and translate classical texts:

Translating Classics: AI systems can translate and adapt historical literary works into contemporary languages, preserving their essence while making them accessible to modern readers.

Examples: The "ReLit" project uses AI to translate and republican classical texts, providing modern translations that retain the original's stylistic and cultural nuances.

This chapter explores the transformative role of AI across various cultural and artistic domains, including music, visualarts, cinema, literature, digital games, media, and translation. AI not only enhances traditional artistic processes but also opens up-new possibilities for creativity and expression.

Conclusion :

the evolving landscape of artificial intelligence (AI), leveraging its capabilities can be a powerful strategy for achieving financial independence and success. Here are some detailed tips for readers on how to effectively use AI to attain financial goals: 1. Take Advantage of Free and Accessible Tools: AI offers a range of free and accessible tools that can serve as a foundation for generating passive income. Many platforms and applications provide entry-level solutions without requiring significant investment. Explore and utilise these resources to get started on your journey to financial independence. Tools such as AI-driven content creation apps, automated trading platforms, and data analysis services can offer valuable assistance at no cost.

2. Continuous Learning: The field of AI is dynamic and rapidly evolving. To stay ahead, it is essential to commit to continuous learning. Engage with training courses, webinars, articles, and other educational resources to keep abreast of the latest developments and advancements. This ongoing education will enable you to harness new technologies effectively and adapt to changes in the AI landscape.

3. Adapt to Technological Changes: Rather than resisting technological changes brought by AI, embrace and adapt to them. This involves updating your personal and professional skills to align with new demands. For instance, familiarise yourself with emerging AI tools and applications that can enhance your efficiency and productivity. Adaptation can provide a competitive edge and open up new opportunities in various sectors. 4. Embrace Creativity and Innovation: AI is a powerful enabler of creativity and innovation. Use AI tools to explore novel ideas and launch ground breaking projects. The digital realm offers endless possibilities, and AI can act as a partner in developing innovative solutions. By integrating AI into your creative processes, you can discover new ways to solve problems and achieve your goals. 5. Consider Ethical Implications: Ethical considerations are crucial when utilising AI technologies. Ensure that your use of AI contributes positively to society and adheres to ethical standards. Avoid practices that may harm individuals or communities. Ethical AI use involves transparency, fairness, and accountability, and it is important to align your AI applications with these principles.

6. Invest Time Wisely: Effective time management is key to leveraging AI for financial success. Clearly define your goals and prioritise AI tools and strategies that align with these objectives. Organize your time to focus on activities and projects that offer the highest potential returns. Strategic investment of your time can significantly influence your overall success.
7. Leverage Social Networks and Digital Communities: Join online groups, forums, and communities that focus on AI and its applications. Engaging with others who share your interests can provide valuable insights and foster collaboration. Learning from the experiences of peers and exchanging ideas can enhance your understanding of AI and help you achieve greater success. In summary, harnessing the power of AI for financial independence involves leveraging available tools, committing to ongoing learning, adapting to technological changes, fostering creativity, considering ethical implications, managing time effectively, and engaging with relevant digital communities. By applying these principles, you can effectively navigate the AI landscape and achieve your financial goals."

www.ingramcontent.com/pod-product-compliance
Lightning Source LLC
Chambersburg PA
CBHW070205230526
45471CB00002B/826